HOW TO DEAL WITH DIFFICULT PEOPLE

Learn How to Identify and Deal With Different Types of Difficult People

(Easy Tips for Dealing With Difficult People)

John Turner

Published by Sharon Lohan

© **John Turner**

All Rights Reserved

How to Deal With Difficult People: Learn How to Identify and Deal With Different Types of Difficult People (Easy Tips for Dealing With Difficult People)

ISBN 978-1-990334-77-1

All rights reserved. No part of this guide may be reproduced in any form without permission in writing from the publisher except in the case of brief quotations embodied in critical articles or reviews.

Legal & Disclaimer

The information contained in this book is not designed to replace or take the place of any form of medicine or professional medical advice. The information in this book has been provided for educational and entertainment purposes only.

The information contained in this book has been compiled from sources deemed reliable, and it is accurate to the best of the Author's knowledge; however, the Author cannot guarantee its accuracy and validity and cannot be held liable for any errors or omissions. Changes are periodically made to this book. You must consult your doctor or get professional medical advice before using any of the suggested remedies, techniques, or information in this book.

Upon using the information contained in this book, you agree to hold harmless the Author from and against any damages, costs, and expenses, including any legal fees potentially resulting from the application of any of the information provided by this guide. This disclaimer applies to any damages or injury caused by the use and application, whether directly or indirectly, of any advice or information presented, whether for breach of contract, tort, negligence, personal injury, criminal intent, or under any other cause of action.

You agree to accept all risks of using the information presented inside this book. You need to consult a professional medical practitioner in order to ensure you are both able and healthy enough to participate in this program.

Table of Contents

INTRODUCTION 1

CHAPTER 1: WAIT, WHAT IS REALLY WRONG? 2

CHAPTER 2: HOW TO DEAL WITH A BOSSY PERSON 9

CHAPTER 3: HOW PRESSURES AFFECT DIFFICULT PEOPLE 14

CHAPTER 4: HOW TO DEAL WITH THE NAGGING, ANNOYING PERSON WHILE STAYING POLITE 40

CHAPTER 5: TYPES OF DIFFICULT BEHAVIOURS 44

CHAPTER 6: ENTER INTO CONVERSATION 63

CHAPTER 7: DON'T TAKE IT PERSONALLY 70

CHAPTER 8: DEVELOPING YOUR INTUITION TOWARDS FRUSTRATION 80

CHAPTER 9: CHANGE YOUR ATTITUDE 88

CHAPTER 10: DEALING WITH OLDER EMPLOYEES 91

CHAPTER 11: THE "ANTI-DIFFICULT PEOPLE" TOOLKIT AND HOW TO LEARN FROM IT 114

CHAPTER 12: A DISHONEST WORKER 124

CONCLUSION 134

Introduction

This book will offer suggestions on how to handle people who are difficult to deal with in your life. We all have someone somewhere who likes to pull our chains and put us on the edge. Read on to see what we will suggest to get that cranky relative on the right track, your nasty neighbor to be your friend, and that coworker who is always miserable to get off your back and just do his/her job.

Thanks again for downloading this book, I hope you enjoy it!

Chapter 1: Wait, What Is Really Wrong?

Problems can be perplexing, and at times can be cryptic. Perplexing problems disturbs and dazes the one in trouble and if proper care isn't taken, the problem might swallow the victim.

Cryptic problems are deep and always hidden that all efforts to locate or get to the root of the problem will prove abortive. It only takes a man of deep wisdom and understanding to unravel the mystery surrounding it.

Before you can conclude or say someone is difficult or hard to get along with, there are things you must look out for within yourself and consider very well in order to carefully discover what is really wrong.

WHO ARE YOU?

This is the number question you must ask yourself. It could be that you are wrong or you are really not getting what is wrong. It could be that you are the cause of the person's attitude towards you. It could be that you are at fault and not the person in question. It could be that you have shortcomings or negative characters that pisses the person off.

The first step to take in dealing with a difficult person is to look within. You must be able to know what exactly is wrong before taking any other step. This will save you unnecessary stress and needless headaches.

During my stay on campus, I had a room-mate who happened to possess a total different personality compared to mine. He was always reserved unlike me that say things and give my comments the ways things are.

My room-mate was someone you can't really touch his things if you want to avoid problems. But me, I was always free with my things and hardly would I be seen complaining about the misuse of my things. I am a jovial type and I joke a lot and hardly do I take things serious, but he wasn't like me. He takes every word as they seem to appear or sound and give back necessary reactions.

Our first few weeks were filled with ups and downs and there were times he left the room for somewhere else just to avoid my untamed jokes that pisses him off and sound annoying to him.

It took us almost three months to understand each-other based on the maturity we that we both later displayed. Of course, it could have been longer.

Mind you, it didn't happen by magic. I sensed I was the main root and cause of the whole problem and I took necessary caution. I knew I was at fault almost all of the times, even if he had his own shortcomings too.

WHAT WERE MY DISCOVERIES?

I discovered we had different upbringing and we grew up under different circumstances.

I sensed he doesn't like his things being touched, tampered with or given to someone else without his consent.

I discovered he has boundaries to joke and will always frown at expensive ones.

I discovered he doesn't joke with money and he likes too much of decorum unlike me that hates boredom.

I noticed he doesn't want the room to be messy, even my own things got to be well arranged. He wants the room to seem untouched or unlived.

I observed that that was his way of life and nothing could change that.

After my discoveries and everything I noticed, I made up my mind to make necessary adjustments and correct my short comings.

I adjusted myself, made amendments and made sure he sensed the change. You know; like I said that he had his own fault too during our misunderstanding seasons. What he did was that I overheard him reporting me to an outsider. I was not happy with this and I hate being reported to someone else. I believe if I offend you you should be able to call me and explain things to me direct instead of telling someone else. So, after I made amendments, I said to his face one thing he did also too of all his faults that pained me to my heart. I poured out my mind and told him what he could have done. And after my complains, he too apologized and that was the end of all our misunderstandings.

It got to a point that other hostel mates and students around started thinking we were actually from the same parents. All these happened just because we have come to understand ourselves; me avoiding his dislikes and he too, avoiding mine.

We saw ourselves just like brothers and lived like two grown adults. We lived for goo d three years without a day of exchanging unpleasant words or having issues.

If I hadn't taken my time to study myself and discover what exactly was really wrong, I could have seen him as a difficult person or someone I couldn't move with at all.

Same thing applies to you too. Before you come to the conclusion of ascribing the word "difficult" or "hard" to someone, check for what is really wrong and make the necessary amendments. It will help you a lot to face the real deal.

However, this might not be true with everyone having the responsibility of dealing with a difficult person. The person termed a "difficult person" might really be difficult indeed. In this case, what must you do? Or how do you go about it especially when it is a must for you? This will lead us to the next chapter- "We are not the same, we are unique".

Chapter 2: How To Deal With A Bossy Person

Spending time with bossy people will surely make your life miserable, if you let them. It is one thing to interact with a manipulative person and another thing to let her control you. Most people are not aware that they are controlling and, more often than not, they will get hurt if you tell them. There are many ways to handle The Manipulator and here are some things that you can try.

1. Give humor a go

Maybe the subtlest way to express your disdain for another person's bossiness is to blurt out half-truth wisecracks. When she demands you to do something, you can tell her "When did you become my mommy?" Or if she is actually your mother you can say, "Mom, the last time I was in the doctor, he said my brain is working well." Just remember to keep everything bright and funny if you want to avoid any misunderstandings or confrontations.

2. Learn to say no

If humor could not handle it, perhaps the best way is to actually say no. Do not give an instant "yes" when somebody is telling you what they want you to do. Deny the suggestion in the most polite manner as possible, but don't apologize for your denial. You can say, "I don't agree with you this time, and I have a better idea in mind that I'd like to try." Usually, a bossy person sees that you are not capable of handling things on your own that is why she is always giving you advice or demands. When you consistently show her that you have your own principles, and you always stand firm by those principles, she will be taken aback and will begin to respect your decisions in due time.

3. Refuse to give in to argument

When you say no, chances are she will get defensive and will try to explain her motives. That all she wants is the best for you and she think you couldn't handle it on your own. Just stay silent. After she has spoken, look her straight in the eye and say no one more time. This time, she might raise her voice and try to start a fight. Do not submit yourself to it and refrain from shouting back. Stay quiet and show through your facial and bodily expressions the firmness of your decision.

4. Be straightforward

Sometimes, you need to be straightforward and tell a person that she is being bossy. This one needs to be done with proper timing, though. Don't embarrass a person in front of other people, for example. Don't talk about her manipulative nature when you can see that she is not in the right mood. It is better to do this in private so that she will realize that you don't have bad intentions.

At times, the suggestions of bossy people are actually sensible and correct. It is just the manner they express it and the expectations they have with it that are making them unbecoming. You can tell her that her ideas are great, but you are offended by the way she is treating you.

5. Check if you are a people pleaser

Lastly, examine your people pleasing tendencies. Are you feeling good when you make another person happy? Are you someone who always needs the approval of others to start doing something? Are you not confident of your own decisions so you ask other people's opinions all the time? Are you agreeing to everyone blindly just to avoid any conflicts or disagreements? If you are these things, you might be a people pleaser, and that is maybe why you are attracting bossy people into your life. Improve your self-confidence by pursuing personal development. Realize that you can't be everything for everyone and you can't please everyone. If you don't look after yourself, other people will take advantage of you all the time.

Chapter 3: How Pressures Affect Difficult People

When pressures in life start to get out of control

How Pressures Affect Difficult People

When pressures in life start to get out of control, a difficult person is born.

Babies are cute even when they start to mess around with things. But

when they grow up, it's a totally different story. The same thing holds true for difficult people.

They start out amusing, even witty, but most of them turn into monsters

later— some overnight.

Life pressures are common. We all encounter them in certain measures,

and the degrees vary each day. They help us mature gracefully, if handled well.

But the moment it controls us, we tend to pass the pressure on to others

and we become a pain in the neck, so to say.

The day you were born, the womb was pressured to the maximum and

your mother had to be rushed to the delivery room.

When you were transferred from the womb into this world, you were

grown through a series of pressures: the pressure to eat, to sleep, to stop

crying, to lie on your belly, to sit, to crawl, to stand up and finally to walk.

Your parents had to force you to do these things as a part of growing up.

Then there's the pressure to eat nutritious things like vegetables and

fruits.

As you continued to grow, you were pressured to talk and pronounce

words properly.

Then, you were sent to school.

There, the teacher introduced new pressures to you to help you learn

more and be updated.

The higher the schooling, the stronger the pressures became. Exams,

projects, recitations, competitions, and the like were introduced to you, because more of those pressures will meet you in the future, they said.

You were born and grown through pressures.

These pressures are all necessary. They are all good. They are designed

to bring out the best in us.

But somehow, when taken out of context or in the wrong perspective,

they become negative pressures that, instead of bringing out the best, bring out the worse.

Pressures ought to be faced maturely. This means the soul (mind,

feelings, and will) is nurtured as pressures are overcome.

But when the ego takes in all the beatings (the soul succumbs to the

pressures), a difficult person emerges and takes over.

Types of Pressures

More often than not, life pressure is the culprit in the emergence of difficult people.

Other types are:

•Peer pressure

when being difficult becomes a trend (glorified in movies and on

TV) and your peers go with the flow.

- Illness pressure

Which is due to a mild illness.

- Disciplinary pressure

Having a difficult attitude is assumed to test the loyalty and

perseverance of subordinates, such as in offices, in fraternities, or in the military. These pressures are often momentary and feigned. Disciplinary pressures seldom result to a bad attitude because it is used to mold the character.

- Overt Pressures

Some pressures in life are obvious. They attack from the outside.

Piled up work in the office, a very demanding boss, deadlines to beat, school or board exams, and a nagging wife are examples of these pressures.

They are often temporary and manageable, cut by rest periods

when the cause of the pressure is allayed. But they show nonetheless, sometimes in slightly heightened degrees.

And yes, some difficult people may also be a result of other

people's being difficult to them.

It's like a vicious cycle - in most cases it is attributable to attitude

transfer. Wrong attitudes can be imparted.

Overt pressures are mostly "skin deep" and can rarely affect the

total person for long periods.

More so, it is seldom permanent.

Bad attitude from this pressure feeds on the periodic onslaughts of

minute pressures, and without such feeding the bad attitude subsides.

But if ignored, such bad attitude may worsen as the ratio of

pressures and rest periods become disproportional. In such case,

the bad attitude recovers quickly from the rest period because the

latter is cut short by a new overt pressure.

For instance, a student is pressured by both financial problems and

the submission of a school project due soon.

He is irked by financial woes and lack of time.

Such double or even multiple pressures produce low LOT. He starts to be prickly with his group mates.

After rushing to finish the project the night before the deadline, the

professor announces a long surprise quiz.

The first pressures have hardly gone by when the second one

comes in.

The rest period is terribly cut short, leaving the battered emotions

unrelieved, and the temperament all the more irritated.

The LOT drops to its lowest point.

When a person is pestered by overt pressure and he has the will to

initially overcome it, he tends to be mildly difficult at first.

LOT slightly lowers.

If symptoms persist and complications are added, he goes halfway

to being extreme. It becomes extremely difficult to stop when the pressures start to really build up.

The LOT dives as a result.

When the pressure increases -- the LOT decreases, and vice-versa.

If a person has control of his LOT and is able to even boost it, he has

mastered the art of self-control and proves to be a strong, patient person we all admire.

Most pressures are uncontrollable, but our levels of toleration are - if we

master them.

And once we do, we are able to help difficult people.

So the game is really all about LOT mastery. And winning the game

means keeping the LOT high up. A high LOT is a sure way of

determining that you are not a difficult person, and a high LOT is a sure tactic for conquering difficult people.

For instance, if any one of these occurs:

- A demanding boss or professor (probably a difficult guy himself)

is appeased,

- A deadline is met

- An exam is passed

and then things quiet down, and the difficult person relaxes and exhibits

tolerable manners.

Often, these ease periods that occur between pressures are relief well taken by him so that he may sometimes be strangely benevolent to people.

You may see him being nice even to people he despises.

He may display acts of kindness or generosity, such as buying everyone

lunch.

But don't be deceived.

Such transitions are temporary. Brace up for another round of

challenges soon.

Overt pressures are at times easy to escape from. Difficult people who

meet such pressures usually resort to other activities to divert attention and be temporarily relieved from the pressures that beset them.

They may busy themselves with some charitable works, games, leisure or hobby.

They may take up a new school course, or socialize and hold positions in

clubs.

Initially, this seems a good way of "channeling energy" to other

"positive" activities, but this is a mere escape route that can change or solve nothing except give short relief.

There are crucial factors affecting overt pressures. Among them are:

•Escapism.

As Karl Marx puts it, anything that diverts attention from the

root cause of a problem is an "opiate."

Escapism is not only an opiate, it drowns its victims in a

whirlpool of falsehood and lies which later transform the person and become real in a victim's eyes.

Many difficult people worsen when they resort to mere

escapism to ward off pressures without confronting and remedying their situation.

The brief relief diminishes in effectiveness. Higher doses of

relief are required to produce a more potent anti-pressure in the same way that antibiotics become ineffective when over-used.

Thus, you often see difficult people becoming harder to

please.

When difficult people resort to escape, they are building their

own world of lies.

Worse, they impose these on other people, so that meaningful

relations are only possible when others adapt to the world of these difficult people.

- Crossing Over.

Some overt pressures, if taken positively, can actually serve

as "stepping stones" to help difficult people overcome their adverse attitudes.

These are called stepping stones because they can slowly

change a difficult person from being difficult to being tolerable or considerate.

It's like crossing over from their false world to the real world.

- Pressure Reversal

When you fight negative tendencies, you reverse the pressure effects and, if done consistently, come out a different person.

This takes a lot of self-control.

Child psychologists say that instead of making a child obey you, you talk

to them in suggestions that make sense based on their interests.

For instance, you can make a child stop running by picking them up and

sitting them in a chair. Or you can explain to them that running might

cause them to stumble and hurt themselves - perhaps them telling them a story about someone injured by running in an inappropriate place.

The child is now focused on ways to avoid getting hurt.

In pressure reversal, a person convinces themselves to always react positively especially in adverse situations.

When you do this yourself, the goal is to not become like the difficult

person you are dealing with.

You don't want to turn into an unreasonably demanding boss someday,

so you assume exactly the opposite attitude your difficult boss shows you.

It takes an apple tree to produce an apple. If you want a banana, you

won't find it on your apple tree.

Likewise, you have to plant within yourself the type of person you want

to become and nurture then nurture the seed. How?

Reason with yourself. For instance, if you are a student facing your final exams, ask yourself: Do you want to pass your exams and get a degree

just to become a rotten character? Do you want to become a difficult

person or a difficult employer yourself?

As you realize the pressure of studying for your exams, or during exam

day itself, and find yourself becoming out of sorts, or testy, persuade

yourself not to give in. Fight it off and bear in mind your goal of becoming agreeably different.

Covert Pressures

Pressures that are imbedded attack from within.

They are the more subtle pressures that make for a more difficult and often defiant or resistant character.

Difficult people born out of covert pressures seem to disagree with

everybody and everything.

They seem to hate the world.

They seldom find respite from their pressures because the pressures are

deep within. It has been built into their system.

Unlike difficult people with overt pressures who still enjoy intermediate

(though temporary) cessation of pressures, victims of covert pressures live a life of being difficult.

They stay hurt and irritated, and are quick to react negatively in many

situations.

Covert pressures are often things in the past that were impressed during childhood, like abusive or damaging words from parents, scenes of

violence, fierce sibling rivalry, discrimination, and persistent financial problems.

Some may be incurred in adolescence or even in adulthood.

Covert pressures either push people to compete for recognition or to

withdraw by blaming others.

These people try to live a dream wherein everything is perfect due to

their designs and doings. They see themselves as heroes who always know the right things to do. They dictate their ways and opinions on

others while fully convinced they are here on a mission to correct others.

People react to covert pressures in 2 ways. They either:

• Compete for recognition.

Covert pressures may goad people to compete for

recognition.

Aching to be recognized is one highly motivational pressure

that has either made or broken lives in history.

A classic example is a boy who, due to poverty, suffered

discrimination and banishment. His relatives made him feel that he would never amount to anything. As he grew up, the boy vowed to do everything to prove his accusers wrong.

He later became a self-made man. Over the years he became

successful materially but his hurt emotions had been imbedded within his ego.

Now, life to him is one big competition.

He constantly strives to show himself as right and others as

wrong.

Of course, he does not announce this as a creed, but without

being aware it becomes the foundation of all he does. It becomes the engine that runs his life, the inspiration that gives him gusto.

So he goes about his daily routine correcting everybody,

giving his unsolicited advice, and making sure everyone listens to him.

After all, he is a self-made man, and people ought to learn

from his example.

And thus the difficult life begins for those close to him and

around him. Of course, any man under covert pressure can opt to react differently and apply a little pressure reversal.

He may still do everything to win in life, but he must also

consider those who are not as successful, and those who do not want to be too successful.

- Withdraw by blaming others.

Covert pressures can also send people to the depths of

despair; and being in a helpless state, they hate others for it.

They may opt to appear defeated and view themselves as a

loser. They may try to prove this to others by refusing to engage in anything worthwhile.

Yet they maintain that they are mere victims of circumstances

beyond control, of which others are to blame.

It is often a life of endless searching for reasons to despair

more. These difficult people see nothing but failure and doom, and urge you to see things likewise.

Yet, they may also opt to appear normal like everybody and

pretend to undertake worthwhile things. But they lead a life

of constantly blaming others for everything wrong and claiming authorship for everything right.

Often, these people will offer little help or suggestion, if any,

unlike those who opt for competition for recognition.

These individuals will only blame and put down people. They

love to see failure mushrooming around people.

They damage the emotional foundations of people. When

ignored, they go deeper and settle in the egos. The ego, or

inner person, is the one within that controls and operates the

person outside. The visible person outside is a mere puppet of the person inside.

When Overt and Covert Pressures Strike Together

The worst scenario comes when both overt and covert pressures attack difficult people.

Imagine a guy with a serious, covert pressure imbedded in his heart

which grows as the years pass by.

Then add the outside pressures that worsen the pressure inside. Hot

steams begin to spill out of breaks in the walls. When the whole thing finally gives way, you have a volcanic eruption in your hands.

In real life, there are such people.

Pressures do wonders to people.

Geological pressures beneath the earth either create violent upheavals. It is the same with pressures on humans.

Pressures can transform people to better and stronger individuals, or they can stir them to chaotic impulses that create deadlier pressures.

People who are able to break through barriers of pressures unharmed

come out like diamonds.

Chapter 4: How To Deal With The Nagging, Annoying Person While Staying Polite

One standard personality that can be difficult to handle is the one who seems to annoy from the moment they walk in the room. It is easy to lose your cool when someone's nagging personality is regularly annoying you. However, there are a few tips that you can follow to avoid letting them get under your skin.

Listen to Them

With some annoying, nagging people, you may have little to no need to interact with them on a daily basis. Others, however, have job functions that overlap or intertwine with yours in some way, so it is necessary to listen to their nagging. In most cases, when someone is nagging you, they have a strong desire to relay some seemingly important message to you, and they will persist in trying to communicate this message until you affirm that you have heard and understood it.

Therefore, pause and listen to the message fully. Give this person your full, undivided attention, and use effective communication skills to affirm that you have heard their message. This may mean saying something along the lines of, "I understand that you have said…." This will help them feel that they have been heard and move along quicker.

Make Sound Decisions

There is a difference between listening to and understanding what someone is saying and following their instructions. Some people may be so irritated with a person that their first inclination is to immediately deny any request that the person has made to them. However, it is important to always make sound, impartial decisions even when you are feeling annoyed. Therefore, while listening to the person, try to consider what the fair, impartial solution is.

Be Firm

Once you have made up your mind, be firm in your resolve. If your decision is counter to this person's wishes, denying their request or failing to follow their instructions may result in continued nagging. Simply state your decision, and offer a small explanation regarding the reason for your decision. It is not necessary or beneficial to engage in a back-and-forth debate about the topic if you have heard the request, and you have made a fair decision.

Create Space

To avoid being subject to continued nagging, it is often necessary to walk away from someone who is nagging. You can and should do this politely and professionally. After you have stated what you need to say, simply tell the person that you have a meeting to get to, a phone call to take or an important file that needs your attention. If possible, walk back to your desk, spend some time in the conference room or head to another area of the office that puts space between you and this person. Dealing with a nagging, annoying person can make you miserable, and your response to their behavior can reflect poorly on you rather than them. Follow these steps to keep your cool when dealing with an annoying person at work.

Chapter 5: Types Of Difficult Behaviours

The saying that everyone says and almost no one believes is that "nobody is perfect". You can disagree with what I say. But, If you think about it long and hard, I am sure you will remember that one person you wanted to be like, or that life you wish you had. Why do you wish those things? Was it because you thought their lives were perfect, or at least maybe you thought their lives were much better than yours.

The one thing that you need to realize is that everyone is essentially flawed; some people are more flawed than others. So there will always be difficult people everywhere.

Realize there will always be difficult behaviours and difficult people

Wherever you go in the world, you will find difficult people who act like they enjoy hurting others. As you cannot escape encountering these people, you need to learn how to deal with them and to communicate with them. Let us identify the different types of behaviours encountered in people. They can be describe them as the following

Aggressive Behaviour

This is when a person is confrontational, angry, pushy and aggressive when they think you have done something wrong. They have a tendency to steamroll over people, without letting them explain or speak. They way to communicate with a person exhibiting such tendencies are

First take stock of what they are getting emotional about.

Get their attention by calling out their names in a calm tone, repeatedly. If that is not enough wave your hand indicating them to stop at the same time.

Once you get their attention, let your response be clear and assertive but calm and uninfluenced by emotions.

Give them some credit for their concern, suggest an alternate solution, and make sure to convey your intent with clarity.

Make sure to let them know that you will not take disrespected.

Passive Aggressive Behaviour

This is often found in people who do not know how to express their emotions or needs very well. They will not tell you to your face the issues they have; instead they act in other ways to sabotage you. They try to make you feel bad about something that they are going through, what you can do to make them less passive is

Make sure to let them know that you can sense the hostility.

Treat them with kindness every time they treat you with hostility.

Make them feel as safe as possible, be kind

Give all the indication of openness and willingness to listen and level with them

If they do open up about the issues they have with you don't try to deny and justify away the issue.

Think long and hard about what you might be doing wrong, offer solution and keep your word.

If you go back on your word and use their response to punish, it is not going to help you or them in any way.

Trolling

This is when someone looks for security in a crowd, avoids direct confrontations, and attacks when people are at a vulnerable spot in the midst of a crowd. This is when a person acts from where they think they are safe, and tries to make you look foolish, or to undermine your work or put you in a spot. These people want the importance, the spotlight, but are usually too scared to attract people's attention. So they envy other people who have the attention and try to put them down.

When faced with someone like that, the remedy is to put the spotlight on them. Bring them out into the open. Confront them immediately when the derogatory or unwarranted comment is made. Never get defensive, instead put them on the defensive by asking for an explanation.

Hold them responsible for what they said, by asking them to elaborate. Don't let them change the topic or divert from it, before they can clearly explain their comment or snipe.

Usually that itself is enough for the person to back down. If you can convince them to explain what they meant without getting emotional or angry, then it may be possible to resolve the issue that they have with you.

If not they will think twice the next time before taking a shot at you.

Narcissistic Behaviour

This is a behaviour often seen in people who are deeply insecure in their own abilities and feel the need to show off. When dealing with these types of people, there is no way you will win an argument with them. If you want to convey an idea to them,

Make it seems like it was their idea all along. If the idea sticks never ever try to indicate that they were not the ones to come up with it.

The best way you can get them to agree with you is to lead them towards the conclusion you want them to have.

Another thing you can do to minimize conflict with them is to let them win. There is no such thing as reasoning it out with them.

For yourself, the best thing you can do is minimize your interactions with them. If they really do value you and care for you, they will examine their behaviour, recognize the issue and try to change. Otherwise, there is no way you can try to change them.

Know-it-all

This is when a person tends to have a one way attitude with information. They are always the ones speaking, they never listen to what others have to say and most importantly, they think they are always right. Admittedly, they do often know deeply about the subject than others. This makes it difficult for others to get across a new idea, as they are very set in their ways.

The way to handle a conversation is to make sure you go well prepared for a discussion with them, suppositions and uncertainties do not work with them.

These people look for ways to discredit your opinions and try to dash the opinion as soon as possible. So being prepared is the key. Hesitation or self doubt will kill the message before it reaches their ears.

Overconfident bragging will lead to a mocking disagreement and immediate discrediting.

The key is to make the conversation collaborative. It is ok to let them think that they have helped you decide the authenticity of the point you wanted to convey.

If you want the person actually listen to you instead of shooting you down, the way to do it is to involve the person in a discussion and convert it into a consultation of sorts.

If a person point blank denies to explaining the reason he does not agree with you, then you might have to let it go. Sometime there are people who do not want to reason with you or act civilized.

Nitpicking

A person is nitpicking if you are criticized constantly, no matter what you do or how much you try to match expectations. These people like to micromanage everything to death and rarely give complements. You sometimes feel that she is makings "mountains out of a molehill." Here are a few steps to deal with the person.

First look at what you are doing, are you making these mistakes regularly, and make sure that you are not the issue in the situation.

If the person treats you and everyone else the same way that will give you just a little relief, that it is not your fault but their own.

If you have a feeling that you have been singled out for the nitpicking session, ask for a one on one meeting, to resolve the issue as soon as possible.

Ask to talk to them calmly without slinging accusations, start with telling them you would like to have a better relationship with them that is not full of negativity. Bring in the topic of the nitpicking gently and request a way that the issue can be resolved, either by compromise or discussions etc.

If this is still not resolving the issue, then try to find a way to reach a compromise with a third party to mediate between the two of you to resolve the issue.

If the situation is something you are facing at the workplace and the issue is affecting your job and work, escalate the issue to the peers to get the issue resolved. Choose this method only after you have made sure that you will be able to get the support you need from your peers.

If you find that nothing works to change the situation, consider finding ways to avoid the person by minimizing contact.

If the nitpicker is closer to home, maybe a partner or a parent, then try to see their point of view, have a good conversation about what is bothering each of you. Try to come up with equal agreeable compromises.

If that does not work, seek professional help who can help you both navigate the issues you are facing.

Unresponsive/Passive behaviour

This is another type of behaviour that people get into when they are usually un-reactive. They tend to agree with everything you say. They never offer their own opinions. This behaviour is usually seen in people who feel insecure in their surroundings, and do not have the confidence to support or voice their opinions. They often need encouragement, a safe non judgmental space. What you can do to handle such a person is

Create a safe place for them to speak the truth, make them feel like their opinions will be accepted without bias.

Do not let them feel that whatever they say will be later used as ammunition against them.

Try to genuinely understand what the person is saying; put yourself in your shoes for a moment by putting your beliefs aside.

Make it known to the person, that they will not lose your regard if they say no to something.

Don't judge them for not agreeing with you or not having the same priorities as you do.

Try to explore the reason for a person's unresponsiveness by guessing and trying to get them to answer. If you find out that they are just private people, and the silence is just their way of self preservation, take note, and back off a little.

If the person has a tendency to flake after saying yes to something, make sure you double check and triple check with them. If the behaviour still continues make to try and find out if there is a reason they are flaking on you. If you still can't solve the issue, give them an ultimatum. Never leave the request open ended.

Indecisive Behaviour

This is when the person is having a lot of difficulty making decisions, often leading to procrastination and unfinished work or promises. These people have a tendency to look for better choices, perfect solutions. Sometimes it can be that they have a fear of saying no to something or someone and end up either agreeing or saying maybe. What you can do to ease this confusion or indecision is basically help them be more decisive.

Make them realize that it is not possible to please everyone in the world, nor is it possible to find a perfect solution.

Consider, if the person reason to not decide immediately has merit and if the issue needs more thought.

Help them learn how you make decision, help them establish a decision making system that will help to make their decision faster.

Tell them that the world is full of imperfections and imperfect decisions and that not taking a decision is worse than taking an imperfect one. This is one of the most important points to get across, as it is what causes the most trouble with them.

Be patient, invest a little time into their thought system, put yourself in their shoes and try to understand their thought process, and look for the merits in it.

Help them navigate their confusions by giving them a defining framework to use, tell them the consequence of not acting.

Histrionic Behaviour

This type of behaviour is when the person always loves to have attention. They often go to any lengths to get it. They tend to find ways to make their lives look like a rollercoaster ride, without any consideration to the people around them. These people will always keep craving more attention, no matter how much of it they get, it is never enough.

The one sure way to give them what they want is to pay attention to them.

You may be unable to avoid these people, if so just listen to them. Don't ever make the mistake of getting involved in their affairs.

The more involved you get the more entangled you will get with their drama

The only thing you can do with such a person is cut strings the first chance that you get and then keep your distance.

Complaining

This is when the person complains about everything constantly. They feel helpless and cannot seem to understand why they suffer so much. They constantly find problems with other people and the world. If you offer them solutions, it does not help them. Instead they will simply find more problems with the solutions. Things you can do to communicate effectively with the person complaining is to first, listen to their problem.

Take note of what they are telling you, if it not specific; ask them to specify the issue.

When people complain, they have the tendency to unload their stress without facing the issue at hand. So tell them to face the issue when you come up with a solution to their problem.

Let them know very clearly what they could do as a part of the solution, and tell them the choices they have.

Often those who complain don't really want to choose a solution as both the solutions are not something they would like to do, so instead they keep on complaining and don't make a choice. For example,

He wants to leave the job that he is working at and go pursue another one in another city, but if he does quit the job and go for the other one, he knows his partner would not approve of it. You have offered a solution to him to have a good discussion with the partner and then decide what is to be done. He does not do it and keeps complaining. Tell him that he already knows what he needs to do.

Set boundaries, and draw a line of how far you are willing to indulge him.

Tell him clearly that you would help him if he is ready to act on the advice. Say clearly that if he just complains without any action, he cannot come to complain afterwards. It will simply be a waste of your time.

The above mentioned behaviours are only a few of the many types there are, but dealing with all of these behaviours involves a few things in common. Maintaining your calm, making sure you are not at fault and them actively listening and responding, and offering solutions.

Chapter 6: Enter Into Conversation

The next step is to engage in conversation. By this stage you should have empathised with the angry person's feelings, listened to their concerns and expectations (or demands), asked clarifying questions, and maybe even identified common areas of agreement. Thanks to your actions, the other person has most probably calmed down and the intense anger has probably been replaced by annoyance, irritation, or frustration.

They should be able to think more rationally and should have calmed down sufficiently to listen to what you have to say. It's now a good time to enter into a dialogue and to start working toward a mutually satisfactory solution. For this step to be effective there are more guidelines for you to follow.

Show that you care and that you truly want to resolve the issue.

Continue to give the other person full attention – don't be distracted.

Use "I" statements when you state your point of view.

Focus on the pertinent facts, rather than opinion.

Look for areas of agreement.

Give them a 'small' win.

Stay in the present. An angry person will often bring up past events and try to draw you in. Maintain your focus on the current issue and suggest to the antagonist that you should both focus on what is the current cause of contention and address one issue at a time.

Don't force proof that you are right and they are wrong as this will only upset them further. Calmly explain your point of view, refer to facts. Make it easy for them to change positions without losing face.

If staying on track is not working, steer the conversation onto a related but less volatile subject. See if you can regain common ground before moving back into the problem.

Bring the conversation back to centre if you get off track.

Tip: Don't tell the person to 'calm down' as this it will quite likely add fuel to the fire. Remember that somebody who is angry is not thinking rationally.

What is the root cause of the anger?

It is important to get to the root cause of the problem instead of just battling the symptoms, otherwise the problem may well resurface down the track.

Use empathetic listening: "Tell me more" "Help me understand". Open ended questions work well here to help find out what's really bugging him or her.

More often than not, anger is shielding another emotion, such as:

Guilt

Hurt

Loss

Anxiety

Sadness

Loneliness

FEAR

The 'Counseling Center, California State University Bakersfield, states that underlying anger is the result of "perceived loss of control over factors affecting important values." The values may be related to pride, love, money, justice, etc.

As an example, maybe a sales person drives across town for an appointment with a prospect, only to find the person is not available and did not phone to postpone. The underlying emotion could be "hurt" (this prospect showed no respect for my valuable time). A different example could be that of a person who uses anger as a tool to make himself/herself feel better.

Some people are very judgemental, constantly blaming others for any issues they face, not taking any responsibility, and getting angry in the process. Their thinking is filled with 'should's' and 'ought's' and 'musts'.

What makes one person angry might be water to a duck's back for another person. It all depends on how they interpret the event, which is influenced by past experiences, which buttons are pushed, and negative emotional associations, etc.

Threatening Event----> How The Event Is Interpreted

If you can identify the root cause of the anger, this helps you to create emotional distance from the anger and better cope with it.

The Value Of an Apology

If the other person's anger is justified, and you – or your business – were the cause of their upset, then take responsibility, which means you probably should apologize. Please note, I said 'probably' should apologize because in a business situation you need to consider whether an apology could expose you to the possibility of liability litigation.

The beauty of a well timed and genuine apology is that it usually has a calming effect and it is a positive step toward rebuilding the relationship.

What is one thing you should not do? Blame and defend actions. This will only serve to make the other person even angrier. So what should you do instead? Ask them what they think you should do to fix the issue.

Verbal Abuse

Don't tolerate verbal abuse, instead what you need to do is discontinue and postpone conversation.

Should the other person become abusive, or threatening, immediately give them a verbal warning that you will not tolerate such behaviour and that you will terminate the conversation if they continue. Let them know you would be prepared to continue the discussion once they have calmed down.

If the verbal abuse does not stop, repeat that you will not tolerate such language, and terminate the conversation.

Chapter 7: Don't Take It Personally

Part of the reason that difficult people create so much trouble is because you tend to take their behavior personally. If you think that people are difficult as a deliberate affront to you and if you take difficult behavior as a sign that people do not like you, you will spend a lot of your life very hurt. The key to dealing with difficult people is to stop taking their behavior so personally.

You need to realize that people are acting out for reasons that are most likely totally unrelated to you. It may be any one of the reasons that I listed above. It may be a completely different reason that no one else knows. But it is probably not directly because of you. Only in rare circumstances is someone's difficult behavior ever targeted at you.

When you stop taking things too personally, you stop stressing yourself out over the behavior of others. You can start the process of nullifying or balancing out others' difficult behavior. There are many things that you can do instead of becoming upset or angry about difficulties with other people. What are some of the things that you should do instead of taking things personally? Take a more constructive approach to difficult people, rather than a hurt and personal approach, so that you can transform difficult interactions into more rewarding ones.

View Difficult People as a Challenge

Do you want to know what sets successful salespeople and entrepreneurs apart from average people? It is all in the attitude. Successful people are far more likely to view difficult people and situations as fun challenges. They welcome difficult people and make it a point to "win" with difficult people. They do not take things personally or give up in despair.

It is important to start viewing difficult people this way yourself. Think about how this is a great opportunity for you to turn someone's attitude around. Focus on bettering the situation, rather than running from it or worsening it.

Empathize

Having empathy makes life so much easier for everyone. As you become empathetic, you become able to understand why people do the things that they do. You become more gentle and caring. You avoid a lot of misunderstandings. It becomes easier to forgive people for their transgressions when you understand what they were feeling when they performed an action.

Try to look at things from someone else's shoes before you rush into any judgments. Changing your perspective is the key to empathy. Consider their recent life circumstances and their personalities.

Consider that you may have triggered them to have a certain reaction. Consider how prepared they may be to handle situations well. If you try to view something through someone else's eyes, you may realize someone's motivation and reasons for acting in certain ways.

For example, someone who has endured an abusive childhood will probably not have the best coping skills for relationship problems. When you two fight, he completely shuts down and stonewalls you. Instead of taking it personally and thinking that he must simply hate you, try to consider how difficult it is for him to handle relationship stress. Give him another chance and communicate your needs with him. "I understand that you hate fighting. But I hate it when you shut down. Can you please talk to me instead of shutting me out?" is something that you could say to this individual.

Try to Find the Source of Difficulty

It is better to be proactive and to approach life from a solution-oriented angle. When someone is being difficult, just drowning in your sense of upset is useless. Rather, it is far more conducive to success if you try to fix the situation. Exploring why someone is being difficult can help you find solutions to their behavior.

You can start by facilitating open communication. Have you ever tried asking a difficult person what is upsetting him or her? Try it and you might be surprised how much he or she will soften. People are not used to having others care. If you appear to care, people will often soften toward you and work with you. They will realize that you are not so bad after all.

Find a Balance

Understand that it isn't your Fault

A major part of not taking things personally is to understand that most of what other people do is not your fault. People have their own problems. They spend most of their time wrapped up in their own issues, so that they have trouble understanding how their behavior affects others. While this is no excuse for rudeness, it clears you of fault when people act difficultly around you.

Some people are also very selfish. They are so focused on their own goals that they neglect to think of your own sanctity and happiness. Don't blame yourself for being weak. Blame them for being terrible to you. You should be more assertive in the future, but do not beat yourself up for being kind and trusting.

Don't Define People

It is easy to judge people based off of their actions. We are often taught to put more value in actions rather than words, and for good reason. The actions of others often speaks volumes louder than their words. However, when someone exhibits some difficult behavior, you might want to reserve judgment for later. People are not always defined by their behavior.

It is common to think, "He is such an asshole" or "She is such a bitch" after observing less-than-desirable behavior in someone. But you should never make such assumptions right away. You should give someone a second chance before you label them and shut them out forever. You may find a great co-worker or best friend in someone, so don't write someone off based on a brief observation. Would you want someone to forever think badly of you just because you had a bad day and acted abysmally once?

Observe someone over time before you make a judgment. Do not base your judgments of someone's character off of one incident. Instead, look at their general demeanor over several incidents.

Avoid Drama

You have a few options when you encounter a difficult person. One option is to silently suffer. Another option is to blow things up and start a fight and a lot of drama. Drama is stressful and it will burn bridges between you and other people. Drama is always best avoided.

It is usually best to appear better than others with your behavior. That way, you will appear reliable and mature and you will not be blamed for anything that happened during a difficult exchange with someone else. Maintain your innocence by being an emotionally detached observer. Do not engage in drama if you want to avoid further problems.

You have a real chance of working things out with someone if you behave in a non-dramatic manner. But if you behave in a dramatic way, you are likely to alienate someone and obliterate all chances of working issues out.

Don't Let It Affect You

Do not let the behavior of other people change who you are. When someone is being difficult, it is human nature for you to want to change. You harden your heart, you become angry, you want to lash out at people. Your moods and your personality can change in the face of opposition.

But understand that the behavior of others actually has very little bearing on your life. Most people who bother you with their rudeness or underhandedness are not actually important in the long run. Ask yourself, Will this person's behavior even matter to me in a year? If the answer is no, then you should not let this person affect you so dramatically. Do not change for him or her. Do not let his or her temporary shenanigans have permanent implications on your life.

Make like rubber and make them glue. Let their words bounce right off of you.

Chapter 8: Developing Your Intuition Towards Frustration

There are always feelings behind the words people say. It only takes a human nature to understand another human being.

This calls for the need to purge your intuition level, in order to understand people's motivation, the reason why they have to nag or complicate situations.

Understanding these facts will help you to avoid situations that might lead to frustrations, and even when people are frustrating you, you will have the right answer to make them stop.

It is very important to sense if the person is just angry with you, insecure, insensitive, frightened, perpetually negative, fearful, hurt, intimidated, etc.

Your level of understanding will ultimately determine how responsive you will become to situations.

Don't confuse intuition

Most people confuse intuition with fearful or wishful thinking. This is because most people tend to be invested on a particular outcome. There is a normal way of seeing things.

You need to go beyond the normal and see things the way they are before you can understand beyond the generalize opinion.

When you feel something, let it be a result of something that is actually happening, not a result of your persistent thoughts, wishes, or fears.

Even though intuition is important, let your solid analysis confirm your suspense. Let your brainpower be manifested, even as you make decisions based on how you feel.

Anticipate outcomes

Let your intuition be built around anticipating certain outcomes. If at the end of your meeting with someone you want a compromise to occur.

Anticipate the situation that will occur after the compromise. Your confidence level will help you make good decisions, say the words that will push even the other person towards your aim.

Before sleep

Make the necessary preparation every night. You need to prepare your subconscious, give instructions to your mind, then go to sleep.

Allow your brain to interpret your decisions, and how you have decided to follow through with the situation.

If nothing changed in the morning, you are definitely taking the right step.

ENVISION

Intuition can be correlated with wise decision-making. When you find yourself alone, envision having a conversation with a wise person, preferably your experienced mentor in that aspect of life.

This is almost meditative and simple to start.

Listen carefully to what your mentor has to say

Determine the questions you want them to ask you. And in different situations, make sure the person is relevant, even in your imaginations.

Do not stop asking questions

People that ask questions often tend to be wiser in the society.

Asking questions and listening to different people answering at the same time will help you to realize and understand the generalized pattern of thinking and how to go beyond normality to do something extraordinary.

It will also help you with ideas on how to conquer the world, and to stay above frustration.

Rinse and repeat

You cannot do something once and expect a good result. Rinsing and repeating even when it comes to decision-making will bring you to the perfection stage.

Sometimes you won't need to think or link something to your emotions before you make a good decision.

The main important thing is the extent of familiarity achieved.

The response mechanisms

Let compassion and clarity lead the way when responding to situations. The trick is to make people admit to their part in causing a particular problem.

Allow them to see the problem that is escalating as a result of their impatience. You don't need to generalize when describing things.

You can focus on remedies instead of the problem. For example, instead of focusing on the words that are coming out of someone's mouth, you can focus on correcting their intonation.

Telling people not to shout on you will bring to light and make them realize what they're doing.

At the moment you will know whether they want to actually make you feel overwhelmed or they are actually concerned about what they are saying. This will give you the clue on how to respond to them.

Examine yourself

Examine how much you need the person and how much this person needs you.

Is it guiltiness or obtuseness, territoriality or resistance?

Focus on your own behavior for the moment. You should be honest with yourself on how you want this to go.

Do you need the argument right now?

How do you want to be seen?

Even when you are not at fault you can always ask the other person how you can make things right.

Go around the person

If you have to go through that person to achieve something, you can always look for alternative.

Let them know of the alternative you have. If they don't want to be disturbed, make them feel like you don't need to disturb them. Ultimately, this is the best way to bring down an ego.

Chapter 9: Change Your Attitude

The third strategy you can use to deal with a difficult person is to change your attitude towards that person. For this, you will need to train yourself to see the person differently, to feel differently when around that person, and to listen to them in a different way.

Take one minute and reflect on the kind of reactions you usually have around a difficult person. Are they healthy for you? Whatever your answer is, the likelihood is that it will not be positive. Difficult people bring out the worst in us. They make us yell, fight, frown, and even feel discouraged. By changing your attitude and your view of a difficult person, you free yourself from the negative reactions.

How to Change your Attitude towards a Difficult Person

How can you change your attitude towards a difficult person? Here is how:

Be proactive not reactive

When you are a reactive person, you tend to blame your circumstances on reality. Here, it is easier to attack a difficult person because you think he or she is the problem. When you change your attitude to become a proactive person, you develop value in yourself. You then start to treat people with respect, and take control of your reactions towards them. When you do this, it does not matter whether you successfully handle a situation, you will always emerge happy and satisfied.

Take responsibility for your feelings

When you argue or get into an abusive confrontation with another person, you normally do this because you are blaming him or her for how you feel. This should not be the case. You are the master of your own emotions and you should not let other people control how you feel, act, or behave. That should be your new attitude.

Chapter 10: Dealing With Older Employees

It's a known fact that younger managers often find it difficult to manage older employees. According to the Chartered Management Institute, 60% of senior managers in the UK report that younger line managers struggle to gain the most out of knowledgeable older workers because they manage them poorly.

Uneasiness about age difference often prevents the two parties from forging productive working relationships. The issues could be on both sides. Research shows that ageism often occurs at line manager level. Think carefully about the choices and assumptions you're making in regard to your older employees. Ask yourself: would I still think that way if they were younger? If not, I'm sorry to say it but you're guilty of ageism.

Assuming older workers will want to retire at a certain age, for instance, or that they will struggle to learn new skills or won't be ambitious near the end of their career can cause untold distress to the workers in question. It doesn't matter if your assumptions are unconscious or even fuelled by a desire to protect an employee's wellbeing; you're lining yourself up for an employment tribunal. In short, you're putting people out to pasture. Would you want someone to do that to your parents?

Of course, there are other reasons why young managers may struggle to handle older workers, not least because of resentment from the latter. Some older employees don't like being told what to do by a young 'whippersnapper'. They may make it obvious via the use of snide comments or supposed jokes, perhaps saying something like, "[Your name] has become important now; he has a badge."

That sort of belittling commentary is often hard to deal with. As is older workers who believe that they are above a certain job in the store or who think they should be spoken to in a certain way because they are older. They may also believe they know more than the new manager because they have more life experience.

The abolition of the Default Retirement Age (effective April 2011) – meaning that employees won't have to retire until they want to – no doubt leaves a lot of managers wondering how to react. Add to that, the fact that a third of UK workers will be over 50 by 2020, and the age issue is fast becoming a big issue for managers. Unless you work in a very young industry, it's something you're going to have to learn to handle.

In one way it's a good thing; managers warn that the UK is facing a skills shortage, with newer employees lacking the knowledge of the older generations;

holding onto, and making the most of, older employees, therefore, is more important than ever before.

Before we talk about how you should manage older employees, let's take a quick look at why some younger mangers struggle so much.

A lot of younger managers are "reluctant" to manage older employees; this could simply stem from a reticence to tell people significantly older than themselves what to do.

Other cases can arise from the manager's own insecurity – these older employees may have been at the company a lot longer than the manager, are usually well respected by the team and, frankly, have a lot more experience than the boss. That's often difficult to reconcile.

Likewise, in some cases, they may also find it hard to find shared ground with an employee significantly older than themself and, if they were brought in to bring a department or outlet up to date, they could experience resentment from them. The older worker could be aggrieved that they have to answer to someone half their age, for instance, or struggle to reconcile to the fact that their boss is possibly the same age as their son or daughter.

While it's often easier to focus on younger employees with whom you have more in common and who you assume may have longer in their career at the company, that would be a mistake.

A good manager, and one who does not feel threatened, recognises the sheer knowledge and experience these older workers possess and works hard to retain it...

How to Manage Older Employees

1. Address them as individuals. Each person has their own aspirations and ideas; don't treat them as a uniform group. Take the time to get to know them and their individual circumstances, just as you would any other employee.

2. Don't make assumptions. Depending on their circumstances, some older workers may want to retire as early as possible, others may wish to wind down slowly while some may have no intention of stepping down for a good while yet.

3. Make the most of their skills. Older workers can be great mentors; being a mentor gives them status in the workplace, is a great use of their skills and helps to ensure their knowledge is not lost when they do leave the workforce.

4. Address any resentment: If the worker is showing resentment towards you, deal with it by calling them into your office and talking to them privately. Point out to

them firmly but respectfully that you are the manager and they need to keep their opinions private. It is not their job to question the company's decisions or your role, at least in company time. In short, treat them as you would any other worker.

5. Use their knowledge: Show the worker that you are the bigger person. Let them know for instance that, rather than feeling threatened by their years of experience, you value it. Ask them to show you how they do x, y or z or point out to them that you all need each other to complement your work. Always consider the best use of your resources, and yes, that does include people.

6. Don't posture: Don't fall into the trap of trying to throw your weight around or being 'the big boss' because you're struggling with older employees; it will rarely impress them. Some of these older workers will probably have been bosses

themselves so they'll see straight through it.

7. Have a conversation. If you have older employees nearing 'retirement age' (though now there technically is no such thing), have an open conversation with them about it. Find out what their hopes and plans are.

8. Be flexible: be prepared to rethink job specs, offer a change of role or different hours (flexitime) for your older workers if they ask or need it.

9. Keep on training: Don't assume that older workers in their 50s or 60s won't want to continue training; failing to include them on new learning opportunities will only help to ensure their productivity falls and their motivation wanes. Give them the chance to learn new skills should they want to.

10. Remember your older workers in group bonding: Think of your older workers when you arrange or attend team building sessions or entertainment events; they may be just as happy in the pub as their younger counterparts, but if they're not, think of something that everyone, young and older alike, can enjoy.

Dealing with older employees can be intimidating for a new younger manager, but the fact is that you have been put into your position for a reason. You just need to remind yourself of that.

If you can harness the knowledge and skills of these older workers in a positive environment, not only do you boost their morale and benefit the company tremendously, you make life so much easier for yourself. Why wouldn't you do it?

How to Deal with Difficult Employees

Welcome to the second part of this book on dealing with difficult employees; in this section, we're going to talk about different personnel scenarios that you may face as you progress through your management career. Whether it's dealing with a lazy employee, a toxic worker, absenteeism, people who request a pay rise or a member of staff with a potential substance abuse problem, you'll find help and guidance here.

As I said earlier, dealing with personnel issues can be some of the toughest work you'll ever have to do, so you want to be informed and up-to-date on the latest laws and management thinking. The solutions contained in this section have been gained from years of my own personal management experience, plus dozens of conversations with my counterparts from across the country.

Before we talk about our first problem employee scenario, it's worth quickly discussing why some employees seem destined to make your working life a hassle.

The first thing you need to understand about difficult workers is that they are often that way because their behaviour has worked for them – or has never been addressed – in the past. The chances are that by being aggressive, shirking responsibility or being out and out lazy, the employee has secured results in the past, whether it be less work to do, a feeling of power or the knowledge that they can do whatever they want and get away with it. That's something you need to tackle. You could say it's like a child; if a child knows it can get attention by crying, it will do so over and over again until someone breaks the cycle.

In some cases, of course, the employee's conduct may not actually be intentional. It could be caused by lack of knowledge, fear, confusion or a lack of motivation.

Your job as a manager is to identify the cause of the problem behaviour as best you can and treat it appropriately.

Whether you are taking over someone else's team where the behaviour was never addressed or it is conduct that you previously sanctioned by lack of action, it doesn't matter. The time to step up is now. When it comes to your problematic employees, you are the one who is going to have to break their pattern of behaviour.

You may very well find that 90% of your time spent managing people is actually taken by just 10% of your employees. You need to be as efficient as you can with that tenth of the workforce to allow you time to spend on the other 90%. As a line manager, it's your job to make sure that each employee knows what the company – and you – expect from them, and that it is their responsibility to meet these expectations.

Of course, it's important to recognise that all employees can be challenging at times; we are all privy to moods, emotions and stress. The employees who are always difficult, however, and show no willingness to change are the ones that you are going to have to work on. These are your truly difficult employees.

It doesn't always follow that they are your least productive or useful members of staff, either; on the contrary, just because someone may be good at their job in many other ways, doesn't let them off the hook if they are always taking credit for other people's work, putting other people down or are aggressive with everyone around them.

In order to turn their offending behaviour around, you must act decisively and swiftly. Don't ignore it because it is easier to do so; that helps nobody, the offending member of staff included.

There's one fact that is worth keeping in mind at all times and you'll find it actually frees you to take a logical view of situations - and that is that no one is indispensible. It's true; everyone can be replaced, even you! All managers have had members of staff that they didn't want to lose; people they assumed the company would miss and struggle without if they left. It could be because they were exceptional at their work or because they had knowledge that no one else had. Well guess what? The company survived just fine! There may have been a period of adjustment but employees and teams are flexible and no one is indispensible. So don't fool yourself that someone is too valuable to lose… they're not. Keeping that thought in mind at all times frees you up to be proactive.

All the information in this sector is designed with one thing in mind; improving the problem behaviour and making that employee a happy and productive member of your team. You have a responsibility to everyone who works for you to give them the chance to correct their behaviour before you take more draconian measures.

It may take more than one meeting, discussion or confrontation to do so, of course, but the results could be worth it in the end. Years ago, I had one problem employee whose attitude made working with her very difficult. I came very close to terminating her employment several times but in the end I persevered. That employee is now a manager herself and is spectacularly good at her job. She credits our time together as the turning point in her life when she stepped away from negativity and inbuilt anger caused by a poor childhood and looked to the future instead.

Success stories like this make the energy involved in dealing with problem employees worthwhile. However, there will inevitably be times when the results aren't quite so positive. It is important to recognise when you are out of your league or cannot solve the problem alone. Some employees may have psychological issues or addictions that you cannot hope to resolve; your best bet if you want to hang onto those staff members is to get them expert help.

It is also important to recognise when things have just gone too far to allow the employee to carry on in your company, in which case you may want to look at termination. In all cases, no matter what the cause, the basic rules on termination should be followed as laid out in our chapter on reprimanding staff.

For now, let's assume that things are not that grave as yet and focus on giving you the tools you need to try and turn around problem behaviour. Let's deal with our first employee...

The Unresponsive Employee

Who they are: This is the member of your team that never seems to listen to what you say; they may barely respond to you when you talk and never do exactly what you ask. Their lack of interaction may frustrate you and their work may suffer as they are too distracted to carry out their duties. They may even blatantly ignore you or don't do things as you ask for them to be done.

What to do: The first thing to ascertain is whether they are actually listening to you. Some people make the mistake of confusing listening with understanding; they assume that if someone listens or acknowledges what they say, they must understand them. Conversely therefore, they assume that because someone doesn't do what they ask, they didn't listen.

Before you deal with the problem of getting their attention, ask yourself a few key questions: Are you presuming he or she isn't listening because they are not doing what you ask? Could it be that they simply didn't understand your request? Are they perhaps listening to you but too afraid to admit they don't really understand what you're asking of them?

That's the first thing you need to work out: are you being explicit with the employee? Just as I warned about the Sandwich Technique in our section on reprimanding, be aware that being too polite and beating around the bush may just confuse or weaken your message.

If understanding isn't the problem, you need to work out why they aren't listening to you. This usually means that you need to get to know the employee better first; I've had employees, for instance, who I thought were unresponsive until I realised that they were actually very poor at doing more than one thing at a time. If an employee is giving their all to a particular piece of work, it may be that they cannot hear anything around them. They may grunt unconsciously when someone tries to talk to them but that doesn't mean they have really taken anything in. Until you get to know the employee, you won't understand that, of course.

It could be, however, that the particular employee's problems run a little deep than that. A key cause of unresponsive employees is lack of motivation. You can't force someone to listen to you no matter how much you may shout to get their attention; what you can do, however, is to create the sort of atmosphere where they are most likely to listen to you. If you have a problem with more than one member of staff in this regard, you need to look at your motivational techniques.

How to Create the Right Atmosphere:

Listen to your employees: If you don't listen to your employees, they are certainly not going to listen to you. This is especially true if there is a perceived problem among the workforce. Having an open door policy where you encourage discussion can yield answers that you never knew you were searching for. Likewise, you might want to have an informal time for listening. Only you can decide if you want to keep a formal boundary between you and your staff, but inviting the team to the pub every Friday after work, for instance, or allowing them to finish an hour early, having a beer together and chewing the fat doesn't mean that you're becoming best buds with them. You don't need to be compromised by simply offering another means of communication. Offer an informal environment in which you are distraction free and listening to them. You may find your answers then. It could be, for instance, that the employee is distracted because of personal problems at home, or he plays on the internet all day because he's bored at work and needs more of a challenge. These are things you can work with.

Don't forget to praise: A team that is never praised becomes demotivated all too quickly.

Know their interests: The more you can tailor your 'message' to the person's interests, the more likely they will be to want to listen to you. Approach it with this in mind to get and keep their attention. If someone hates maths, for instance, don't talk to them in facts and figures; they probably switched off long ago. You may reach them, however, if you talk about a project in terms that inspire them.

Timing, of course, is everything. Don't expect someone's undivided attention if you try to talk to them when they're busy serving a table of 30, or running late for a delivery. Use your intuition and approach them at the most opportune moment. If you have doubts that they heard you or actively listened to you the first time, bring it up again to double check.

Likewise, if you are an authoritarian boss – do as I say, now! – be aware that you may be alienating your team with every order that you bark. According to the Chartered Management Institute (CMI), most managers in the UK are authoritarian, secretive and bureaucratic – and that's not a good thing. High rates of employee sickness and absence result. Four in 10 people also report leaving jobs because of bad management, with nearly half (49%) happy to take a pay cut to avoid overbearing managers.

Finally, if this is a problem across the team, take a quick look at your own behaviour. Could it be contributing? Is what you are saying important and purposeful, for instance? Do you get right down to the matter at hand, or is it a chore to wait until you finally get to the point? Busy employees can't spare the time to listen to you just to boost your ego; likewise, if you give out your instructions in and amongst a whole host of 'nothingness', it's likely that they will have switched off some time ago and miss them entirely.

Assuming you try all of these things and the problem still persists, you're going to need to talk to the employee concerned. If he or she still shows no sign or intention of improving, you may be forced to consider their long-term future with the company. First, of course, you must give them the formal and verbal warnings needed to cover the legal issues involved in termination.

Chapter 11: The "Anti-Difficult People" Toolkit And How To Learn From It

The "Anti-Difficult People" Toolkit

As you go through life, you will, time and again, be faced with one or several difficult people -- at work, at school or sometimes, at home. What do you do?

Listen Carefully. Instinct will tell you to shut your ears and not let these people get to you. This can sometimes be good, but if you're shooting for a long-term defense, you'll want to be aware of who or what you're dealing with.

The thing with difficult people is that more often than not, they simply need to be understood. Difficult people succeed or become worse when people react negatively to them. When you turn to give them your fullest attention - even for just a moment - you end up giving them what they want, making them less hostile, even if it's just for a day.

Besides, everybody likes a good listener. When you make these people your friends, it becomes easier for you to reach out to them.

Don't Be Hasty. Remember how difficult people thrive in the way people react? When you encounter these people, try not to give in to your instincts. Stop first, and think about how you will react. By doing so, you are able to take control of the situation because you get to decide what course of action to take. It only takes a few seconds of your time to think about what you should do in order to save your entire day.

Remember to Put Yourself First. Taking the time to do something to help difficult people can be a noble act, but don't ever do it at the cost of your own well being. Sometimes we get so caught up in the "selfless act" of pleasing these people to appease them, but you end up losing more respect, not only from yourself, but also from the other people around you. Sometimes you have to put your foot down and disagree with these difficult people, not because it's the best way to go, but because the damage they can do to your self-esteem would be a bigger blow.

Remember, you can't help others if you don't help yourself first.

Laugh. There are experiences in life that you would one day look back to and laugh. Why not make this one the kind you would just laugh at today? Encountering difficult people can be seen as a bad experience, and they can be the kind you can just laugh about.

Of course, this is not to say that you should laugh at these people. That's just mean. But what you should do is to laugh at the reality that some people are just the way they are. In these instances, the right perspective is your best defense.

As the old saying goes, "don't take life too seriously, because nobody ever gets out of it alive."

Don't Blame Yourself. Nothing in this world is ever within your complete control. Corollary to #4, keep in mind that sometimes, bad things just happen. And when things go bad, and everybody gets mad, you need to secure yourself the truth that will keep you sane: that it's not your fault (assuming, of course, that it is not your fault), and that someone was just being difficult.

This mindset is particularly important for those difficult people that you just can't live with anymore. It will be your key to moving on from a toxic relationship or quitting the employment of a control freak boss.

These five tips are pretty basic. If you master them, you're already halfway there.

Avoiding the Pitfalls During Interaction

You've learned the do's. Now here are the don'ts:

Do Not Generalize Difficult People. The worst thing that you could do to a difficult person is to always assume he or she is up to no good. When you look at a difficult person and say "oh, it's him/her again," you're not different from someone who just ignores that person.

Sometimes we forget that these people are good for something too. If he or she is a co-worker, there has to be a reason why he or she is there, right?

For example, what if the control freak actually is an expert at a specific task that he or she is taking command? Should you deny control just because the person is a control freak?

Or what if the toxic person really does have a good reason to be angry for once? Are you going to just ignore the rants because Mr. Toxic is just being Mr. Toxic again?

Do Not Be Mean. They are the difficult ones, not you. Sure they have issues, but they are otherwise normal, imperfect people, just like you. Every now and then their bad side will rear its ugly head, but you should be nice to them on any other day. These people are still family or friend too, and developing some kind of festering dislike towards them is just going to make YOU as bad as them.

They are difficult people, not impossible. So what? That doesn't mean you have to be too. Don't be a baby about it and be mature when you relate with these people.

Do Not Underestimate Their Potential. Studies have shown that people with personality disorders can be really smart or very competitive people. This could be the case with most difficult people.

For instance, the narcissists can be very competitive and ambitious, which means that they are likely to do their best when entrusted with work. If you look beyond the ugly parts, the pessimists or even the toxic people can be good sources of criticism (assuming you learn to sift through the negative comments).

Since you can't get rid of these people, you might as well find ways to be able to benefit from them, right? Plus, by tapping their positive side, you can help them feel more secure about themselves, which can do wonders even for the most difficult people.

Learning from Difficult People

There's always something you can learn from others, and that includes the difficult people too. Sometimes it's so tough to look beyond the facade of being difficult that we forget that we can get something good out of them as well. Here are some of the values we can get from someone who is being difficult:

Self-awareness. Remember how you always have to be in tune with your emotions so you can prepare yourself for difficult people? That requires a lot of self-awareness, which is a very useful life skill.

Self-control. Yes, this is a very obvious value that you can learn from this type of folks. In fact, it goes hand-in-hand with self-awareness. And the best part about learning self-control is that it branches out to other life skills, such as tolerance and patience.

Forgiveness. You are definitely going to learn to create and give out a lot of this when you know how to cope with difficult people. Seeing as how aggression should never be a resort in most cases, you're going to need to let go of a lot of damage that difficult people could potentially do. Of course, this does not mean that you should go to the extent of saying that it's okay for people to bully or exploit your kindness. But, more often than not, you're going to want to just let go and learn from each experience, since there's no point in crying over spilled milk.

Compassion. The thing about understanding a person is that it requires you to genuinely be concerned with another person's welfare. When you take time to understand a person better, you get to see how much help that person needs. As you step into another's shoes, you will be more aware that these people just need a bit of care and understanding.

These are just some of the things you can pick up from even the most difficult of people. But the more important part is that all these values you develop from coping with difficult people are actually essential to most of your daily living. Whether you're looking to get better at your job or want to make more friends, these qualities can only help you become better at facing other challenges in day to day living.

Learning to Avoid Becoming a Difficult Person

Perhaps the most unique lesson you can learn from difficult people is how not to become difficult yourself. When you see how other people behave negatively, you get a really good example of how not to relate with other people.

These encounters can give you an opportunity to reflect upon yourself: are you prone to doing the same things you've disliked someone else for?

Chapter 12: A Dishonest Worker

Who they are: Everyone tells a little white lie now and again but a dishonest worker is something else entirely; as their manager, it can be a very delicate situation to handle.

Dishonest employees may tell lies about their whereabouts, make excuses as to why they couldn't get to work on time, blame others for their lack of productivity, take the credit away from other people when they haven't done the work themselves and even lie outright about certain situations.

I've heard stories of managers who have had employees lie to them about family bereavements or imaginary surgeries that meant they needed a week off work with very little notice. The employee obviously isn't worried about bad karma! In more extreme cases, a dishonest employee may steal from the company, at which point you need to part ways. The stealing may or may not be in their true nature but they have overstepped a line and you can never trust them again.

What to do: The difficulty when dealing with an employee you suspect may be lying about their outside activities is that you cannot legally investigate his or her claims outside the place of employment; you can't legally ring around the hospitals in your area, for instance, trying to find out if he or she really is having that hernia repair. You may be suspicious based on his or her previous behaviour, but you can only investigate cases of deception or dishonesty as they relate to the office or work environment. The first thing you should obviously do if the employee claims they are ill is to demand a doctor's note and follow up on it. But what can you do if they lie about other things that you cannot ascertain?

How should you deal with someone who consistently tells lies or stretches the truth?

First, separate fibs or a little white lie (mostly harmless) from a more serious lie that will need to be tackled. You can, for instance, give a little bit of leniency to your good performers who only occasionally stretch the truth. If they exaggerate about the delays on their way into work once in a while, it's probably not a sacking offence. Employees may tell fibs to save face or to save their relationship with you.

Only you can decide when the lying is chronic enough or serious enough to have to tackle. Someone who repeatedly comes in late and always has an excuse or who continually tells lies about the work he or she has done cannot be allowed to continue in their deception.

You are going to need to sit down with them and discuss the issue. Before you have the discussion, however, you are going to need to investigate and gather as many facts as you can. You should plan the meeting ahead of time, preparing what you will say, what the response might be and what your counter response will be in return. Be prepared for an emotional reaction and have your facts and evidence ready to produce. If the deception is serious, you may need to take legal advice.

Always confront the employee in private and be upfront; don't hint at the problem or insinuate what the issue is. State the problem, briefly and succinctly and then allow the employee the chance to state their case. Consider what they say carefully. You may want a HR manager to sit in on the meeting.

If you are keen to keep the employee and 'turn them around', you need to try to come to a mutual agreement moving forward. It may be that the employee can shed some light on why they have been acting the way that they have that goes some way to explaining or offering a solution to the problem.

Be sure to state clearly what the consequences will be if nothing improves. You could mention suspension or termination. If he or she continues to tell lies and claim credit where it is not due, you may have no choice but to start termination procedures.

Make sure you document the entire conversation. If this is the first time you have had to speak to the employee and it is not a very serious offence, it doesn't have to be a formal note as yet. Write a note to yourself reminding you of the discussion and agreements that were made and keep it somewhere safe where you can refer back to it if necessary. If the problem continues, you will need to make this documentation formal.

Dealing with a liar is never easy. Try to avoid using the L word in your discussion if you can; he or she will no doubt rear up at being called a liar, even if it is true! Always create a positive and honest work environment to counteract the opportunity or need to lie to you; be truthful with your staff, never lie to them and make it clear that you expect the same in return. Encourage them to tell the truth on all matters.

If you suspect many of your team are lying to you, you need to ask yourself why. Could it be that your management style is so severe that they never want to get on your bad side, or they are even scared of telling you the truth? If that's the case, you are the one who is going to need to change.

If a worker is found to be stealing, that is usually an immediate sacking offence and may even involve calling in the police. Speak to your immediate supervisor or HR immediately that you discover the truth and seek legal advice on what to do.

A Toxic Employee

Who they are: The term 'toxic employee' refers to an individual on your team or in your department that can be dangerous or poisonous to the morale of your team. A toxic employee can spread negative energy throughout a workforce, fostering antagonism and resentment, subtly or overtly infecting their co-workers with their own bitterness.

A toxic employee may be one who always subtly complains about everything and suggests a sinister ulterior motive to whatever the company does, or the passive-aggressive worker who backbites and then plays the martyr to the hilt when they are called on their behaviour by the manager. Passive-aggressive employees express their aggression in passive resistance; they avoid direct conflict and resist the demands of others by being stubborn and sullen, deliberately inefficient and procrastinating.

The true danger of toxic employees is that they can contaminate others; vulnerable employees can get caught up in the net of negativity and struggle to get out. In some cases, they may not even be aware of how they are being used, believing they are simply agreeing with a colleague as opposed to forming a harmful coalition with a toxic employee. A toxic employee can turn other people against you; they may be able to get other members of staff on their side or influence opinion about you by badmouthing you to others.

A manager can't afford to let the toxic employee spread their tentacles too far because the costs to morale and company productivity can be dramatic. Employees face a negative environment every time they come into work.

The signs of a toxic employee can include:

☐ A decrease in morale and productivity

☐ An antagonistic manner and outlook

☐ Frequent personal attacks to others

☐ An increase in negative comments

☐ Arguments between the employee in question and others around them

☐ A strong sense of frustration from the toxic employee

☐ A sense of tension in the workplace

☐ The employee or employees caught up in the toxicity will be unwilling to go the extra mile, such as work overtime or stay late, and will be vocal in encouraging others to refuse also

☐ They will also be unwilling to help others

Examples include an employee who always complains about their work, who makes snide comments about you or the company, who 'jokes' about issues while making it obvious they are serious or who is constantly miserable and brings everyone down around them. They may also nit-pick on other employees and generally foster a bad environment.

So, if you suspect you have a toxic individual among your staff, what can you do? Ignoring it isn't an option; the negativity will only cast a pall over your remaining employees.

Conclusion

Thank you again for downloading this book!

I hope this book was able to help you to begin the process of learning how to deal with difficult people.

Thank you and good luck!